Successful Group Work

13 Activities to Teach Teamwork Skills

Other Books by Alphabet Publishing

50 Activities for the First Day of School
Walton Burns

Classroom Community Builders
Activities for the First Day & Beyond
by Walton Burns

On the Board
200 *Fast, Fun & Easy Warmer, Filler, and Fast-Finisher Activities*
by Walton Burns

We are a small, independent publishing company that specializes in resources for teachers in the area of English language learning. We believe that a good teacher is resourceful, with a well-stocked toolkit full of ways to elicit, explain, guide, review, encourage and inspire. We help stock that teacher toolkit by providing teachers with books of practical and useful activities and techniques.

* * *

Sign up for our mailing list on our website, www.alphabetpublishingbooks.com, to stay in touch, find out about our new books, and for deals and giveaways you won't find anywhere else.

Successful Group Work

13 Activities to Teach Teamwork Skills

PATRICE PALMER
OCELT, M.Ed., M.A.

Successful Group Work
13 Activities to Teach Teamwork Skills
by Patrice Palmer

Copyright © Patrice Palmer 2017

ISBN: 978-0-9977628-4-6 paperback
      978-0-9977628-5-3 ebook

Library of Congress Control Number: 2017942072

All rights reserved. No part of this book may be reproduced, introduced into or stored in a retrieval system, or transmitted, in any form, or by any means (electronic, mechanical, photocopying, recording, or otherwise) without the prior written permission of the copyright holder.

Edited by Walton Burns

Country of Manufacture Specified on the Last Page
First Printing 2017

Published by:
Alphabet Publishing
1204 Main Street #172
Branford, Connecticut 06405 USA

info@alphabetpublishingbooks.com
www.alphabetpublishingbooks.com

Contents

Introduction	1
Getting to Know Each Other Activities	
Activity 1: Stand Up If...	10
Activity 2: Getting to Know Your Group Members	12
Activity 3: Establishing Ground Rules	14
The Benefits of Teamwork	
Activity 4: Word Lists	18
Team Building Activities	23
Activity 5: Team Challenge	24
Activity 6: The Tower Building Activity	26
Activity 7: Working in a Group, Strengths and Weaknesses	29
Teamwork Skills and Strategies	
Activity 8: Assigning Roles in a Group	32
Activity 9: Consensus Building	35
Activity 10: Resolving Conflict	37
Reflection and Evaluation	
Activity 11: Journal Writing	42
Activity 12: Self Reflection Activity	45
Activity 13: Final Evaluation	48
Conclusion	51
Appendix: Forming Student Groups	52
References	54
About the Author	55

This book is dedicated to my mentor, Linda Gross. I had the privilege of learning from Linda when I worked in Hong Kong. She pushed me to do things outside of my comfort zone. Although it was difficult at times, I am grateful for her support and belief in my abilities as a new teacher.

Thank you, Linda.

Introduction

The activities in this book make up a complete course to teach students the teamwork skills they need to work effectively in groups. It is designed for teachers in any subject area who want to use group projects in their classroom and want to prepare their students to work effectively in teams.

Group work has a number of benefits. During my 20-year career as an ESL/EFL teacher, and TESL Trainer, I have used group work countless times. Group work increases student talk time. It gives students a chance to interact with each other and negotiate meaning, providing opportunities for authentic conversation between students. Groups do better at tasks because they share resources and strengths while compensating for weaknesses in each other. When students are proficient at group work, you can assign them more complicated and interesting tasks and projects.

However, you cannot just say to students, "Form a group and work on the task" without putting the time and energy in ahead of time to teach teamwork skills. Without those skills, we all know what can happen. One or two students end up doing all the work. The rest of the group barely participates, meaning they don't learn. Or the students end up working on the project separately, missing the point of working as a team. The activities in this book emphasize the benefits of teamwork so that students will want to work together.

In other cases, some students may believe that they have nothing to contribute, while other students feel that they can do it all themselves. To prevent this, activities such as Tower Building and Assigning Roles in Groups help students understand that everyone has something to contribute to a project. Students also learn how to organize groups successfully and the value of contributions from different sources.

In some cases, a disagreement may tear a group apart. That's why this book also has activities that target consensus-building and conflict resolution. In fact, students will learn that while disagreements can be difficult, there can also be positive outcomes from conflict.

It may seem time-consuming to implement the activities before students begin working together, however preparing students in advance will help to ensure a successful outcome.

Why Use Team Building Activities?
Team building activities demonstrate different aspects of team behaviors and get students to think about what is essential in order to reach their desired goals or outcomes. Team building activities can also help students think about how certain behaviours contribute to the success of the project. And how other behaviours can obstruct the success of a project or goal. Students will learn positive behaviors from this book such as good communication, problem solving skills, trust, and taking advantage of the strengths of each team member.

Team building activities improve communication skills. The activities outlined in this chapter are practical, experiential, and interactive, providing students with interesting ways to understand what teamwork skills mean, why they are important, and how these skills can be developed for learning, employment and life. Team building activities are also fun. They develop motivation to work in groups.

It is important for students to understand that their teamwork skills are not only developed in dedicated activities like those described in this book. Teamwork skills can, and should be, developed and practiced within their course work. These skills will help students succeed in their studies and their life. As students learn how to work effectively in teams, this should help make your job as teacher easier and more rewarding.

What are Teamwork Skills?

Employability Skills 2000+ published by the Conference Board of Canada are "the skills you need to enter, stay in, and progress in the world of work—whether you work on your own or as a part of a team. These skills can also be applied and used beyond the workplace in a range of daily activities"[1].

Teamwork skills make up one third of those Key Skills. In fact, teamwork skills are so important to our students' futures, that they are called Employability Skills by the US Department of Education.

The activities in this book target the teamwork skills identified by The Conference Board of Canada. The list below shows the skills most strongly targeted by each activity, although students will be practicing a variety of teamwork skills in every activity.

1. **Stand up If . . .** recognize and respect people's diversity, individual differences, and perspectives

2. **Getting to Know Your Group** recognize and respect people's diversity, individual differences, and perspectives

3. **Ground Rules** understand and work within the dynamics of a group

4. **Word Lists** plan, design, or carry out a project or task from start to finish

5. **Team Challenge** contribute to a team by sharing information and expertise

---

[1] *Conference Board of Canada, Employability Skills 2000+ http://www.conferenceboard.ca/topics/education/learning-tools/employability-skills.aspx*

6. **Tower Building** contribute to a team by sharing information and expertise; select and use appropriate tools and technology for a task or projects

7. **Working in Groups** be flexible: respect, be open to, and supportive of the thoughts, opinions and contributions of others in a group; recognize and respect people's diversity, individual differences, and perspectives

8. **Assigning Roles in Groups** lead or support when appropriate, motivating a group for high performance

9. **Consensus Building** be flexible: respect, be open to, and supportive of the thoughts, opinions, and contributions of others in a group; accept and provide feedback in a constructive and considerate manner

10. **Resolving Conflict** understand the role of conflict when appropriate; manage and resolve conflict when appropriate

11. **Journal Writing** continuously monitor the success of a project or task and identify ways to improve; improve communication skills

12. **Self-Reflection** develop a plan, seek feedback, test, revise, and implement

13. **Final Evaluation** develop a plan, seek feedback, test, revise, and implement

How to Use This Book
This book contains 13 activities that teach and develop students' teamwork skills. It is designed for teachers who want their students to improve their teamwork skills before participating in a group

project or other group work. You can use these activities individually to practice a particular teamwork skill. However, this book works best if your students go through all 13 activities, starting before your students begin their group project. This will set your students up for success in group work.

The timing of the activities is somewhat flexible. Some activities clearly work best if they are done before a group project. These include the activities in the Getting to Know You and The Benefits of Teamwork Section. You may want to do these in the first week of class or the week before introducing a group project.

Others such as the Team Building Activities and Learning Teamwork Skills Activities can be done before students begin their group project. However, you could also do them parallel to the group work, giving students a chance to realize what they are learning in their teams. The Reflection and Evaluation Activities work best during or after the group project.

In addition, as students work in groups, you may notice that they could benefit from revisiting some of the activities. Feel free to go back and repeat some of the activities, giving students a chance to reinforce specific teamwork skills. Many of the activities are short enough that they can be done in the first half of class, leaving the second half for group work.

As you go through the activities in this book, it is important to explain the instructions clearly to the students and to check their understanding of the instructions before starting the activity.

For each activity, remember to take time to fully explain the expectations you have from students, as well as the goal of the activity. Some students prefer to work on their own so teachers may have to "sell" the idea of a group project by making students aware of the benefits of teamwork (Activity 4: Word Lists is a good place to start).

Each activity is followed by a set of debriefing questions. Please do not skip these. It is essential that students have a chance to discuss how the activity enhanced their understanding of teamwork and their role as a team member.

As you prepare each activity, and then evaluate the session, you can use these objective statements to guide you:

After this lesson, students will:

- understand and discuss what the benefits are in developing their teamwork skills

- learn and apply a useful teamwork skill

- experience and demonstrate examples of what effective teamwork is

- understand clear guidelines regarding teamwork before they are expected to work together

- apply the guidelines for effective teamwork

- be provided with feedback on their teamwork skills in order to reflect on successes and areas for improvement

The activities in this book will set up your students for success in groupwork by teaching them team building skills. Your students will then be ready for any group project or task you give them. They will then be able to apply the skills learned in your class to other projects in school and eventually in the workplace.

Please feel free to connect with me.
If you have any questions about this book, please contact me at teslinstructor@gmail.com. Let me know if you want to receive my free newsletter of weekly wisdom blog posts as well.

Join the Successful Group Work Facebook page (https://www.facebook.com/groups/106059966623292) to share resources and success stories.

Find me on Twitter (@eltwisdom) and LinkedIn (https://ca.linkedin.com/in/patricepalmer1).

For additional teaching resources for ESL/EFL teachers, please visit my website at www.patricepalmer.ca.

And to learn more about being a teacherpreneur, go to www.teacherpreneur.ca.

Getting to Know Each Other Activities

As with any new classroom situation, there may be some students who feel anxious about working with people they do not know. Start off with a few icebreakers to help students relax and get to know each other.

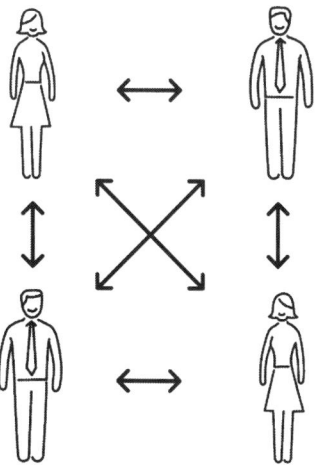

Activity 1: Stand Up If...

Not only does this activity require very little preparation, but students enjoy it.

TIME:	*5 minutes*
MATERIALS	*a set of 8-10 statements prepared in advance*
TEAM BUILDING SKILL:	*recognize and respect people's diversity, individual differences, and perspectives.*

Procedure

1. Explain to the class that you will read off a statement. If they can answer "yes" to the statement, they have to stand up.

2. You can also reverse the activity by having students start off standing and sit down if they can answer "yes" to the statement. The statements should be worded to help students learn interesting facts about each other and develop an awareness of the similarities and differences in groups.

Here are a few statements that work well.

Stand up if...

you are an only child

you can play a musical instrument

you can speak more than three languages

you have been to Japan

you like chocolate

you like coffee

you are the oldest in your family

you are the youngest in your family

you like to cook

you think learning English is difficult

you have a pet

you can swim well

you like working in teams

you liked this activity

Activity 2: Getting to Know Your Group Members

Students should now spend some time getting to know the members of their groups. For this activity, give students about 6-8 minutes to work in pairs interviewing each other.

You may want to prepare some questions in advance. You can also brainstorm some questions from the class. A set of three to four questions should be enough.

Once the interviews are completed, each student should then introduce the person they interviewed to the whole class. Students like this activity because it is much easier to talk about someone else than it is to talk about themselves.

TIME:	*6-8 minutes for interviewing, 12-15 minutes for reporting to the group*
MATERIALS:	*a set of questions developed by the teacher or by the students*
TEAM BUILDING SKILL:	*recognize and respect people's diversity, individual differences, and perspectives.*

Procedure

1. Elicit some questions from students or provide a list of questions. Some examples are: Where do you live? What program are you enrolled in? What is your career goal? What is one hidden talent or skill that you have?

2. Let students know that they have 3-4 minutes in order to conduct the first interview. Students should ask each other the questions you prepared or elicited and take notes on the answers during the interview.

3. After 3-4 minutes, tell students to switch so that the other student is asking questions.

4. When the pairs have finished, each student will introduce their partner to the group. If you have a large group, ask each student to report back one interesting fact to share.

Activity 3: Establishing Ground Rules

At this point, students are ready to begin working on ground rules. It is always good practice to have students formulate the rules at the beginning of any new course and this idea can be modified for group projects. The goal of this activity is to give students a chance to discuss how they prefer to work together and establish accepted principles for dealing with each other. This activity was adapted from an activity in the *Washington Youth Voice Handbook* by Adam Fletcher.

TIME:	*20-25 minutes*
MATERIALS:	*Flipchart paper, markers, Blu-Tac or mounting putty or tape*
TEAM BUILDING SKILL:	*understand and work within the dynamics of a group.*

Procedure

1. Explain the importance of having clear ground rules that everybody agrees on to the group. Tell students that ground rules should be clear and simple. The purpose of ground rules is to ensure a good learning environment for all students.

2. Elicit some potential ground rules from students. If students are not familiar with setting ground rules, teachers can provide some examples:

    - We all share the workload.
    - We all contribute our ideas.
    - We do not disrespect other people or their ideas.
    - We listen attentively without interrupting.

3. When students have an understanding of ground rules, put students into groups (preferably their teams for their group projects) and ask them to set some ground rules.

4. Have one presenter from each team share their ground rules with the whole class. Once the first group has presented, ask subsequent groups to add to the list to avoid repeating items already listed.

5. Ask one team member from each group to volunteer to type up the list of ground rules and give each member a copy before the next class.

Debriefing Questions

- How can ground rules help your team members work together effectively?

- What should you do if you find that ground rules are not being followed by some team members? (You can note these down and use these examples during Activity 10: Resolving Conflict).

The Benefits of Teamwork

In order to get students to work well in teams, they need to understand the benefits of being in a group. The Word Lists Activity illustrates the benefits clearly by having students attempt a task alone and then in a team.

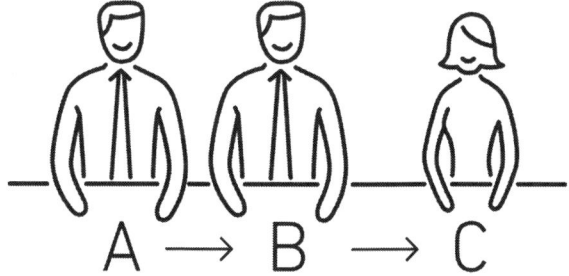

Activity 4: Word Lists

This experiential activity is helpful in getting students thinking about the advantages and challenges of teamwork.

TIME:	*20 minutes*
MATERIALS:	*2 word lists on PowerPoint Slides or flipchart paper. Sample word lists have been included in this activity. However, you may wish to use your own examples. You could also elicit 15 words from the class. Choose words that are appropriate to your students' language level.*
TEAM BUILDING SKILL:	*plan, design, or carry out a project or task from start to finish*

Procedure

Start off the lesson with a brainstorming session where students think of the benefits and the challenges of working in teams. If students have not had a chance to work in teams in an academic setting before, they may wish to think about other examples such as in sports, extra-curricular activities, or their families.

Then tell students they are going to participate in an activity that demonstrates how working in a team can be more efficient than working alone.

Procedure for the Individual List:

1. Tell students that they are going to practice working on their own and then working as part of a team. Let students know that they will have a chance to discuss this activity when it is completed.

2. Tell students that you will show them a list of words for one minute. When the time is up, they will have one minute to write down as many words as they can remember.

3. After the minute is up, ask students for a count of the number of words they remembered. Do this in a way that demonstrates visually the power of teamwork.

4. Start the count by asking students who remembered at least one word to stand up. Hopefully, the whole class will stand.

5. Now, ask students who remembered more than two words to remain standing, while the others sit down.

6. Then ask students who remembered more than three words to remain standing while the others sit down. Build up to higher numbers, so that at the end, the students who remembered the most words are still standing.

Procedure for the Team List

1. Tell students that they will repeat the same exercise with a new list of words. Now they will have only 30 seconds to look at the words. However, this time they can work as a team to recall as many words as possible.

2. Give students 2 minutes to discuss a strategy they might use to get their best results as a team.

3. Then, follow the same procedures as for Part 1, but as a team they have only 30 seconds to make their list.

4. Ask them to write their list on the second column on their paper and then add up how many words they remembered as a team..

Sample Individual Word List

road	building	cell phone
library	walking	look
school	foot	students
brown	music	computer
book	computer	college
water	Singapore	bus

Sample Team Word List

moon	cat	project
teacher	movie	rain
headache	window	spider
television	lunch	swimming
table	calculator	Asia
pizza	coffee	test

Debriefing Questions

- Which list is more complete – the list you recalled as an individual or the list you recalled as a team? (Ideally, the list compiled as part of a team should be the longer list). Why do you think that is the case?

- What were the advantages and disadvantages of working on your own and as part of a team?

- What strategy did they use to get their best results?

Follow up the discussion by addressing the elements of what makes a team work well together. Some examples might be more effective working as part of a team, lighter workload, and shared brainpower to name a few.

Team Building Activities

Team building activities provide team members with an environment in which they can understand the assets and skills they possess when working as a team, as well as the challenges of working as a team. The activities in this section provide practice in various aspects of working as a team so that students can reflect on the experience and learn the value of teams.

Activity 5: Team Challenge

This quick team building activity is fun and can create a lot of noise so be prepared.

TIME:	*5 minutes*
MATERIALS:	*List of items to be displayed on a flipchart or PowerPoint slide. You can also dictate the list to the class. The list of items should be easily found in your classroom or students' backpacks/purses.*
TEAM BUILDING SKILL:	*contribute to a team by sharing information and expertise*

Procedure

1. Put students into groups.

2. Display or dictate the list of items.

3. Tell students that their group will work together to find the items on this list, as quickly as possible.

4. All items need to be displayed on their team's table. When they have found all the items, the team shouts, "Finished! Teamwork!"

5. The other groups should continue until all the groups have finished. Make a list of the order in which the groups finish so you can check the items group by group when all groups have finished.

6. The group that finishes first (and has all the correct items) are the winners.

Debriefing Questions

- How well did your team work together?

- Did your team have a strategy before you started on this challenge?

- What skills did you need in order to finish the task?

- What role did you play in this activity?

- How do you think this activity might be similar to your group project?

- How can you apply what you learned in this activity to your group project?

Sample List of Items:

pen

marker

book

gum

sunglasses

coin

hairbrush

photo

phone

student card

Activity 6: The Tower Building Activity

This team building activity is a fun and useful activity for students to learn about the benefits of teamwork. They must engage in problem-solving, project planning, and dealing with the pressure of working with deadlines. This task requires students to build a three-dimensional, free-standing tower using only the materials provided by you. You can also find a wide variety of other building tasks online. This version was adapted from an activity in the *FireStarter Youth Power Curriculum: Participant Guidebook* by Adam Fletcher.

TIME:	*12 minutes for planning*
	8 minutes for building
	10 minutes for debriefing
MATERIALS:	*You will need a yardstick or tape measure*
	Each team will need:
	3 sheets of flip-chart paper
	4 full-size paper plates (stiff, not flimsy)
	4 paper cups (12 or 16 oz.)
	4 regular drinking straws
	3 feet of masking tape
	1 pair of scissors
TEAM BUILDING SKILL:	*contribute to a team by sharing information and expertise, select and use appropriate tools and technology for a task or project, communicate effectively to complete a task*

Procedure

1. Tell students they will be building a 3-dimensional, free-standing tower from the materials you provide. Explain the rules:

- During the planning phase, they cannot touch any of the materials.
- They may only use the materials you give them to build the tower.
- When finished, the tower cannot be supported by any object or person.
- When finished, the tower cannot be attached to anything such as the floor, ceiling, a wall, or a team member.

2. Give students the specifications for their tower:
    - The tower must be at least 5 feet tall
    - It must be able to withstand a moderate breeze (as blown by you).

3. Because of the complexity of the instructions, check for understanding before beginning the activity.

4. Have one representative from each team come and get the materials they need. Write the list of items on the board or have them written out on flipchart paper before the class starts. Check that teams do not try to use anything besides the materials you provide.

5. Give teams 12 minutes to plan how to build the tower. After the planning phase, give them 8 minutes for building.

6. When the time is up, measure each tower and blow on each one lightly to see if it stays up.

Debriefing Questions
- How was your experience working with the people in your team?
- Did you complete the task but neglect relationships?

- Was everyone in your group involved?

- What did you do together which had most impact on your becoming a team?

- What did you do, personally, which most helped the group to become a team?

- What can you learn about teamwork from this activity that you can apply to your group project?

Activity 7: Working in a Group, Strengths and Weaknesses

Before students begin working as part of a group, have them look at their members' strengths and weaknesses. This will help students to get to know each other better. It will also establish respect by building an awareness of the diverse talents and capabilities in the team. This will provide a basis on which to assign roles, which will be discussed in the next activity.

Since many people are uncomfortable talking about their strengths and weaknesses, structuring the questions in the right way is paramount. Teachers may wish to assign this as homework so students come to class prepared with their answers.

This activity was adapted from an activity in the *Washington Youth Voice Handbook* by Adam Fletcher.

TIME:	*30 minutes*
MATERIALS:	*Prepare a handout or ask students to provide paper/notebook and write down the statements.*
TEAM BUILDING SKILL:	*be flexible: respect, be open to and supportive of the thoughts opinions and contributions of others in a group;* *Recognize and respect people's diversity, individual differences and perspectives.*

Procedure

1. Ask students to finish the following statements:

    I enjoy doing . . .

    I can make . . .

I know something about . . .

Some of my strengths are . . .

Some things I would like to be better at are . . .

Other people tell me that I am good at...

2. Ask students to share their statements with their group members.

3. When the groups have finished, ask them to prepare a master list of what was reported.

4. Ask to see where the strengths/areas for improvements are in each group member. How can these strengths be best used for the benefit of the team?

Debriefing Questions

- What did you discover from this activity?

- Did the group members possess all the same strengths or different strengths?

- How can a group best utilize the strengths of its members?

- How can this activity help your group in deciding who will do which tasks as part of your group project?

Teamwork Skills and Strategies

Like the previous activities, the activities in this section give students practice working on a team. However, these activities also teach specific skills and strategies to work effectively in teams, including assigning team roles and conflict resolution.

Activity 8: Assigning Roles in a Group

If a group is going to be successful and finish a project on time, there are some essential management tasks that group members need to fulfill. Assigning roles is a helpful way to see that those tasks are fulfilled.

TIME:	*20 minutes*
MATERIALS:	*images of roles to help students brainstorm*
TEAM BUILDING SKILL:	*lead or support when appropriate, motivating a group for high performance.*

Notes on Roles

When your students begin their group project, you can either assign the roles, or have students volunteer for a particular role. You also must decide if the members will keep these roles for the duration of the project or if the roles will be re-assigned periodically. Generally speaking, it is a good idea, however, to rotate the roles so everyone gets a chance to develop specific skills. For projects lasting just a few weeks, this would not be a good strategy.

Before roles are determined and assigned, make sure that you have indicated the number of students for each group. Four to five students per group is a good number.

Procedure

1. Once you have determined the number of students in each group, ask students to think about either 4 or 5 roles that would be beneficial in keeping them on track. Have students think about a workplace and the types of jobs/roles that people have.

2. Another way to complete this activity is to provide the class with 4 or 5 roles and ask students to think about 2 – 3 things that this person will do as part of the group project.

3. Make sure that before the class ends, each student has been assigned a role. Have the Note-taker write down each student's role and provide a copy to you.

Roles for Group Work

Chairperson
in charge of the discussion

Makes sure everyone speaks and contributes their ideas

Gives the team direction

Manager
Responsible for ensuring that all the materials needed for the session are ready

Timekeeper

Keeps track of the time in class and during project meetings

Keeps everyone on track

Keeps a close eye on due dates, deadlines, and timelines

Note-taker

Responsible for taking notes on discussions and tasks to be completed

Provides copies of notes to team members in a timely manner

Activity 9: Consensus Building

This activity will give students an opportunity to practice brainstorming techniques while learning to come to a consensus, which is important for successful group work.

TIME:	*20 minutes*
MATERIALS:	*An ordinary object such as a paperclip, a spoon, or a pencil.*
TEAM BUILDING SKILL:	*be flexible: respect, be open to and supportive of the thoughts opinions and contributions of others in a group;* *Accept and provide feedback in a constructive and considerate manner*

Procedure

1. Explain that the purpose of brainstorming is to come up with as many ideas as possible in a short period of time, using the following rules:

    - Students should attempt to list as many ideas as possible within the given time limit.

    - During the brainstorm, no one says whether the ideas are good or bad, workable or not workable. All ideas are acceptable. After the brainstorm is finished, they will be able to evaluate all the ideas.

2. Show the object to the class. Ask students to suggest all the things that they could do with the object other than its purpose (for example, a spoon is used for eating so students must list

an alternative purpose). Encourage students to be creative with their responses. Give students 2 minutes for this part of the task.

3. When time is up, ask each group to read out their ideas. Write their suggestions on the board, noting any duplicate ideas.

Debriefing Questions

- What can you learn from sharing/pooling ideas?

- What was your strategy for getting your creative juices flowing?

- Was it difficult not to evaluate other people's ideas while brainstorming?

- What is a good way for teams to decide or come to a consensus on one idea?

- Is this a strategy that you can use in your teams when you need to make a decision?

Activity 10: Resolving Conflict

Students working in teams may find themselves struggling with conflicts, and unsure how to resolve them. This activity will provide students with an understanding of conflict, how to analyze conflicts they have experienced, and ultimately of how to work together to find solutions.

I adapted this from a lesson that used to be available on the website at the PBS TeacherSource (www.pbs.org/teachers).

TIME:	*30 minutes*
MATERIALS:	*whiteboard or flipchart paper*
TEAM BUILDING SKILL:	*Understand the role of conflict when appropriate; manage and resolve conflict when appropriate*

Procedure: Part 1

1. Write "conflict" on the board. Ask students for their definitions of the word.

2. Next, explain to students that conflict is a part of life. We all experience conflicts at home, at work, in school, and in other aspects of our lives. Conflict can be negative, but it can also be positive. Conflicts with other people may be uncomfortable, but trying to solve them can often make us think differently and may lead to new ways of looking at things. Tell students that at the end of this activity they will learn how to resolve conflict.

3. Have students work in their teams to discuss some examples of conflict. Give students about 5 minutes for this part of the activity.

4. Record their ideas on the board using a word web format. Draw a circle around the word "conflict" and then write the words students associate with conflict at the end of lines radiating from the circle.

5. Discuss the contents of the web by asking:

    - Are there any generalizations we might make about our associations with the word "conflict"?
    - Why are most of our associations with conflict negative?
    - Are there any benefits of conflict?

Some possible ideas for benefits include: It can shape our thinking so that we have new ideas, Sometimes it can bring us closer to another person once we've worked it out.

Procedure: Part 2
In pairs, students take turns talking and listening as they discuss conflicts in their lives.

1. Give each person 2 or 3 minutes to respond to the following prompt:

    What was a recent conflict you experienced? Who was involved? What did he or she do? How did it turn out?

2. After each partner has had a chance to speak, ask the class:
    - What was it like to share about a personal conflict?
    - Did your partner really listen? What made you think so?
    - What kind of body language shows that someone is listening (eye contact, facing the speaker, leaning forward)?
    - What were the outcomes of some of the conflicts?

This activity can also be modified by making a list on the board and having students choose one conflict. They should work in groups to discuss a strategy for dealing with the conflict.

Debriefing Questions

- Do you feel better prepared to handle conflict in your teams after this activity? Why or why not?

- What do you still need to know about conflict resolution?

- Do you think that there is anything your team could do to avoid conflict?

- How do you think your team might resolve conflict?

Reflection and Evaluation

Reflection and evaluation are the most frequently neglected steps in group work. However, they are critical to improving teamwork skills and ensuring better results in the future.

Activity 11: Journal Writing

Journal writing is an excellent way for students to communicate with their teacher about their thoughts and feelings on how the group project is progressing. In assigning journal topics, the teacher may assign a topic or students can be given a list of topics to choose from. Instructions for journal writing should be clear and specific, especially if this is a new learning task for students. It is important that students are encouraged to present their thoughts, observations and feelings as they relate to their own experience as a team member. Teachers will be able to gain insight into any problems that team members may be having in terms of the group work.

TIME:	*Varies*
MATERIALS:	*Pen and paper or tablet or laptop computer*
TEAM BUILDING SKILL:	*continuously monitor the success of a project or task and identify ways to improve*

Journals are written accounts of events, descriptions of people, places or things, or expressions of feelings or ideas. They can be used to integrate experience by providing a medium through which students can share problems, explore ideas, focus on a particular theme, and reflect on their personal growth.[2]

Students can use them to communicate with you. Some students are more willing to write about problems than discuss them face to face. You can choose to respond in writing or in a personal discussion, or to hold a class session on an area of particular interest or concern to students.

---

2   *from TRANSITIONS: A Practical Guide to the Workplace, Teacher's Resource Book, Linda Winder, 1992, Maxwell Macmillan Canada, Inc.*

Journals can reinforce the students' communication skills, giving them practice in writing, even writing in a different language. Finally, journals can become the source of further reflection, thoughts, or new opinions about issues or situations in the group project.

Managing Journals
Here are some simple guidelines to keep in mind to consider when deciding how best to manage students' journals.

Students should be given opportunities to choose their own journal topics as well as complete the ones you assign. This will enable students to write about a current problem, question, or observation that has meaning for them.

The confidentiality of the students' journals is critically important. Journal writing entries should be kept private and confidential. The contents of journals should never be discussed with others or open to public view or otherwise shared without the student's permission. Make sure that students know that their journals will be confidential. This may help students to be more honest and open in their writing.

Finally, journals should not be marked or corrected. Instead you should write encouraging and supportive comments to students.

If you are teaching a course with an online component, ask students to submit entries online. Consider assigning a small grade to ensure completion of this activity.

Depending on your workload and class size, reading several journal entries may be difficult. Another option is to give students ten minutes at the end of class to write the answer to one of the questions below on a slip of paper. Stand at the door and collect each slip. Remember to say thank you to each student as they hand in their paper.

Journal Writing Topics
The teacher can either assign a topic or allow students to write on the topic of their choice. Here are a few topics to get you started.

> I work my best when . . .
>
> I'm glad I'm involved in this group project because . . .
>
> Questions I still have are . . .
>
> The thing that I find most difficult is . . .
>
> This week I learned . . .
>
> The hardest part of this week was . . .
>
> I need help with . . .
>
> Some problems I am having are . . .
>
> This group project is making me feel . . .

Activity 12: Self Reflection Activity

This activity will give both students and teachers an idea of how students are progressing in their group project. Students often need to be "taught" what self-reflection means, and provided with examples.

Use the notes below to help students with self-reflection.

TIME:	*15 – 20 minutes. (this can be completed during class or outside of class)*
MATERIALS:	*2 copies of the evaluation form for each student*
TEAM BUILDING SKILL:	*Develop a plan, seek feedback, test, revise and, implement*

What does it mean to self-reflect, and what are the benefits? The purpose of self-reflection is to think and to develop awareness of barriers or challenges that are holding us back. By reflecting, we delve into problems or situations, and develop solutions or clarity. At first you may be hesitant to self-reflect, but if you persevere, I am confident that you will quickly see the benefits.

Self-reflection is an exercise in introspection so we can learn about ourselves in order to achieve self-awareness. Being self-aware means developing the ability to look within ourselves to understand our thoughts, beliefs, emotions, motivations and our personality in general. Self-awareness is important because once we are able to figure out aspects about ourselves, we can make positive changes necessary for a better sense of well-being.

Everyone is able to self-reflect. However, it may not be a habit that we use in a conscious way. Self-reflection is most helpful when we are trying to make sense of how diverse ideas fit together, when we are trying to relate new ideas to what we already know, or when new ideas challenge what we already know. Self-reflection is about getting to the core, gaining insight and a better perspective, and ultimately finding solutions.

Procedure

1. Discuss with students the importance of evaluating oneself. You can use the notes above to help you guide the discussion. Ask students to complete the form honestly.

2. Give students a specific due date for the evaluation form. Take one copy and make sure students keep the other copy.

Self-Reflection on the Group Work

Name: _____

Read each statement and put a check (✓) in the YES box or the NO box. Effective team members should have more checks in the YES box.

		YES	NO
I am	using good communication skills		
	being a team player		
	demonstrating a positive attitude		
When gathering information for the project, I have:	contributed as a team member		
	provided my information on time		
	completed the task to the best of my ability		
When working with my teammates, I have:	tried to resolve any conflicts		
	accepted teammates' opinions and comments		
	appreciated teammates' ideas and effort		
	tried my best to work on all activities		
When producing the work, I have:	produced work on time according to the team's schedule		
	been conscientious		
	been creative		
	used original ideas		
	cited my sources correctly		

Activity 13: Final Evaluation

Students should prepare a final evaluation based on the group project. This evaluation form gets students thinking critically about their contribution and the contribution of their team members.

TIME:	*20-30 minutes (can be completed outside of class)*
MATERIALS:	*2 copies of the evaluation form for each student.*
TEAM BUILDING SKILL:	*Develop a plan, seek feedback, test, revise and, implement*

Procedure

1. Review this handout with students at the beginning of the group project so that they understand the expectations. However, do not distribute the forms until a few weeks before the evaluation form is due. Let students know that their evaluation is confidential and will not be shared with other students in the group.

2. Give students a specific due date for the evaluation form. Allow at least a week for students to reflect on the experience being part of a group.

3. It is a good idea to assign a mark for this assignment to ensure that it is completed.

Name: _____

Individual Evaluation on the Group Work/Project
Project Name: _____

Answer the questions below honestly.

List your tasks and responsbilities for this project	
At home	In class

How many hours did you spend on this project	_____ hours	
Did you like this project?	☐ Yes	☐ No

Why or why not?

If you could change anything about this project, what would it be and why?

What did you learn through doing this project

The grade I think I earned on this project is a	_____
I earned that grade because::	
In the future I would choose to work with the same people on a group project	☐ Yes ☐ No
Why or why not?	
Imagine you were doing this project for work and your team was paid $50,000 total. How would you divide the money up among your teammates, based on how much each person contributed to the project?	
Name:	Pay $
Name:	Pay $
Name:	Pay $
Name	Pay $
Name:	Pay $
Total	$50,000
If you were an employer, would you hire your group for a workplace project?	☐ Yes ☐ No
Why or why not?	

This form was adapted from "Improving Student Responsibility for Learning and Behavior through Ownership Development" by Mitchell Keith, Bonnie Puzerwski, and Patricia Raczynski.

Conclusion

Group projects can be exciting. They involve a lot of work for teachers and students. However, the payoffs are numerous. I hope these activities in this book have helped you prepare your students for successful and meaningful group work. Your students have learned a lot about the benefits of working on a team, planning and implementing a project, valuing the strengths in themselves and others, dealing with conflict, and reflecting on their own progress. And these skills will serve them in future classes, their work, and beyond.

At the end of the project, remember to celebrate students' achievements. Share specific examples of how much they have developed their Teamwork Skills. You may wish to prepare a checklist using the Employability Skills Framework on Teamwork Skills so that students can see how much they have improved in developing their teamwork skills.

Remember as a teacher, it is important for you to reflect on your teaching and role in student group work or projects. Make notes and write down your reflections to help you in facilitating future group projects. What do you think went well? Are there some activities that you would modify? If so, write them down now while they are fresh in your mind.

Finally, do you have a success story that you would like to share or photos of students engaged in some of the activities in this book? Please add them to the Successful Group Work Facebook group at https://www.facebook.com/groups/106059966623292/

If you have any questions about this book, please contact me at teslinstructor@gmail.com. You can also write to let me know if you'd like to receive my free newsletter of weekly wisdom blog posts.

Appendix: Forming Student Groups

During my experience as a teacher for more than 20 years, I have found that students prefer to form their own groups. This works well when students know each other but I have discovered that in many post-secondary level classes, students come from a variety of programs and therefore may not know any one in the class. If this is the case, ensure that all students are included. No one likes to be that student who is left out.

It is important to give students time in class to form groups. Then collect a list of names for each group. Students like to give their groups names so consider this as well. Again, make sure that before students leave the class every student is part of a group. You may need to facilitate this especially if students are shy or uncomfortable approaching groups.

Teacher-Assigned Groups
If you wish to assign students to groups, here are a few ways to do this:

1. **Randomly mix groups.** Provide a list of names to each group. Inform students that the groups are fixed. If you allow for even one or two changes, this will defeat the purpose of pre-assigning groups.

2. **Groups in same program.** You may wish to have students from the same program forms group however this may leave out a few students who are enrolled in programs that are not represented by others in the class.

3. **Groups in different programs.** This ensures a mix of ideas and perspectives based on different post-secondary programs.

4. **Groups according to interest.** If you're aware of different interests of your students or if students are choosing their own group work topics, you might want to put them together and have them connect their common interest to the task.

5. Alphabetical grouping. Group students based on the alphabetical order of their names or your class list.

Random Groups
Here are some ways to form random groups:

1. **Use popsicle sticks or pull names from a hat.** Write students' names on popsicle sticks/paper, shake them up in a cup, and pick out the number of names you want in a group. (This works well with smaller classes. I have had more than 50 students in some college communication courses). If you use popsicle sticks, keep them handy so when you ask the class a question, you can pull out a stick and ask that student to provide an answer.

2. **Count off.** This is one of the fastest ways to get students into groups.

3. **Use a pack of playing cards.** Pass out cards and group students based on having similar or different suits, black or red cards, cards in a specific order, the same numbers, or any other values you assign to the deck. Again, this only works if you have less than 52 students in your class.

References

In writing this book, I relied on a number of sources. The definitions of teamwork skills from the book were taken from The Conference Board of Canada's Employability Skills 2000+ website at http://www.conferenceboard.ca/topics/education/learning-tools/employability-skills.aspx. The Department of Education of the United States has a similar list at http://cte.ed.gov/employabilityskills/

The Washington Youth Voice Handbook and the *Firestarter Youth Power Curriculum: Participant Guidebook*, both by Adam Fletcher, are great sources of teambuilding activities. Some of the activities in this book were adapted from activities in those sources.

Jennifer Moon's book, *A Handbook of Reflective and Experiential Learning* is a good book about self-reflection. Linda Winder's Teacher Resource Book, *Transitions: A Practical Guide to the Workplace* is a great source of information about journaling. I also recommend "Improving Student Responsibility for Learning and Behavior through Ownership Development" a Master's Action Research project by Mitchell Keith, Bonnie Puzerwski, and Patricia Raczynski, published at http://files.eric.ed.gov/fulltext/ED435955.pdf.

About the Author

After 20 years in the ESL classroom, I have made the successful transition to teacherpreneur. A teacherpreneur is an educator who combines his/her creativity, skills and expertise to develop products, resources and/or services for additional income. In short, I make a living doing the things that I love: teaching, writing courses and ELT materials, blogging, as well as teaching online courses. And writing books like the one you are holding in your hands right now.

As a teacher, I have taught students from 8 to 80 years in a variety of educational environments such as English for Specific Purposes (ESP), English for Academic Purposes (EAP), Business English, and taught communication courses at post-secondary institutions. During my 7 years in Hong Kong, I was responsible for developing English Language curricula for secondary schools, vocational training programs and summer intensive courses. I also developed and delivered workshops for teachers of English related to teaching and learning. The idea for this resource resulted from my work with teachers and students in Hong Kong.

I have a Master of Education degree in Teaching, Learning and Development from Brock University, Canada; a Master of Arts degree from the Ontario Institute for Studies in Education (OISE) of the University of Toronto and a Bachelor of Arts degree from York University, and an OCELT qualification.

As a teacherpreneur, I have written several online courses, including a 10-module course for students in Saudi Arabia, a course on Anger Management for a psychologist, a course in increasing one's well-being. I also have an e-book, *an A-Z Guide: How to Survive and Thrive as a New ESL Teacher* (coming out in a new edition from Alphabet Publishing soon) and *Dream Beyond the Classroom: The*

Essential Teacher to Teacherpreneur Toolkit. I also write bi-monthly blog posts for two ESL/EFL websites including my own weekly blog posts.

I am a certified trainer (CTDP) and I have a coaching credential with the Centre for Positive Psychology in the USA. I am also TESL Ontario certified and accredited as a TESL Trainer for Methodology and Theory, and accredited as a Practicum Supervisor and Academic Coordinator.

* * *

Connect with me

If you have any questions about this book, please contact me at teslinstructor@gmail.com. You can also write to let me know if you would like to receive my free newsletter of weekly wisdom blog posts. Or find me on Twitter and LinkedIn.

For additional teaching resources for ESL/EFL teachers, please visit my website at www.patricepalmer.ca.

And to learn more about being a teacherpreneur, you can check out my resources at https://www.teacherpreneur.ca/

Made in the USA
Columbia, SC
20 June 2025